JOURNAL BELONGS TO

TRAVELING EQUIPMENT

- ☐ VISA
- ☐ PASSPORT
- ☐ TICKETS
- ☐ ID'S
- ☐ CREDIT CARDS
- ☐ CAMERA
- ☐ MAP
- ☐ CHARGER
- ☐ MEDICINES

HOTEL RESERVATION _____

PLACES TO VISIT

- ☐
- ☐
- ☐
- ☐
- ☐
- ☐
- ☐
- ☐
- ☐

- ☐
- ☐
- ☐
- ☐
- ☐
- ☐
- ☐
- ☐
- ☐

FOOD TO TASTE

- ☐
- ☐
- ☐
- ☐
- ☐
- ☐
- ☐

- ☐
- ☐
- ☐
- ☐
- ☐
- ☐
- ☐

my travel story

PLACE AND MEMORIES _____

_____

_____

_____

_____

_____

_____

_____

_____

_____

_____

FOOD I TASTED _____

_____

_____

_____

PLACE TO RECOMMEND _____

_____

_____

_____

_____

_____

my travel story

INTERESTING STORY HAPPENED TO ME

my travel story

PLACE AND MEMORIES _____

_____
_____
_____
_____
_____
_____
_____

_____
_____
_____
_____

FOOD I TASTED _____

_____
_____
_____
_____

PLACE TO RECOMMEND _____

_____
_____
_____
_____
_____
_____

my travel story

INTERESTING STORY HAPPENED TO ME

PLACE AND MEMORIES _____

_____
_____
_____
_____
_____
_____
_____

_____
_____
_____
_____

FOOD I TASTED _____

_____
_____
_____
_____

PLACE TO RECOMMEND _____

_____
_____
_____
_____
_____
_____

my travel story

INTERESTING STORY HAPPENED TO ME

PLACE AND MEMORIES _____
_____
_____
_____
_____
_____
_____
_____

_____
_____
_____
_____
_____

FOOD I TASTED _____
_____
_____
_____

PLACE TO RECOMMEND _____
_____
_____
_____
_____
_____

my travel story

INTERESTING STORY HAPPENED TO ME

_____
_____
_____
_____
_____
_____
_____
_____
_____
_____
_____
_____
_____
_____
_____
_____
_____
_____
_____
_____
_____
_____
_____
_____
_____
_____
_____
_____

PLACE AND MEMORIES _____

_____

_____

_____

_____

_____

_____

_____

_____

_____

_____

_____

_____

FOOD I TASTED _____

_____

_____

_____

PLACE TO RECOMMEND _____

_____

_____

_____

_____

my travel story

INTERESTING STORY HAPPENED TO ME

PLACE AND MEMORIES _____
_____
_____
_____
_____
_____
_____
_____

_____
_____
_____
_____

FOOD I TASTED _____
_____
_____
_____

PLACE TO RECOMMEND _____
_____
_____
_____
_____
_____

my travel story

INTERESTING STORY HAPPENED TO ME

my travel story

PLACE AND MEMORIES _____

_____
_____
_____
_____
_____
_____
_____

_____
_____
_____
_____

FOOD I TASTED _____

_____
_____
_____

PLACE TO RECOMMEND _____

_____
_____
_____
_____

my travel story

INTERESTING STORY HAPPENED TO ME

my travel story

PLACE AND MEMORIES

FOOD I TASTED

PLACE TO RECOMMEND

my travel story

INTERESTING STORY HAPPENED TO ME

PLACE AND MEMORIES _____

_____

_____

_____

_____

_____

_____

_____

_____

_____

FOOD I TASTED _____

_____

_____

_____

PLACE TO RECOMMEND _____

_____

_____

_____

_____

my travel story

INTERESTING STORY HAPPENED TO ME

my travel story

PLACE AND MEMORIES _____

_____
_____
_____
_____
_____
_____
_____
_____

_____
_____
_____
_____

FOOD I TASTED _____

_____
_____
_____
_____

PLACE TO RECOMMEND _____

_____
_____
_____
_____
_____

my travel story

INTERESTING STORY HAPPENED TO ME

my travel story

PLACE AND MEMORIES _____

_____
_____
_____
_____
_____
_____

_____
_____
_____
_____
_____

FOOD I TASTED _____

_____
_____
_____
_____

PLACE TO RECOMMEND _____

_____
_____
_____
_____
_____

INTERESTING STORY HAPPENED TO ME

my travel story

PLACE AND MEMORIES

_____

_____

_____

_____

_____

_____

_____

_____

_____

_____

_____

_____

_____

FOOD I TASTED

_____

_____

_____

_____

PLACE TO RECOMMEND

_____

_____

_____

_____

_____

_____

my travel story

INTERESTING STORY HAPPENED TO ME

PLACE AND MEMORIES

_____

_____

_____

_____

_____

_____

_____

_____

_____

_____

_____

_____

FOOD I TASTED

_____

_____

_____

_____

PLACE TO RECOMMEND

_____

_____

_____

_____

_____

my travel story

INTERESTING STORY HAPPENED TO ME

my travel story

PLACE AND MEMORIES _____
_____
_____
_____
_____
_____
_____
_____

_____
_____
_____
_____

FOOD I TASTED _____
_____
_____
_____

PLACE TO RECOMMEND _____
_____
_____
_____
_____
_____

my travel story

INTERESTING STORY HAPPENED TO ME

PLACE AND MEMORIES _____

_____

_____

_____

_____

_____

_____

_____

_____

_____

_____

_____

FOOD I TASTED _____

_____

_____

_____

PLACE TO RECOMMEND _____

_____

_____

_____

_____

_____

my travel story

INTERESTING STORY HAPPENED TO ME

PLACE AND MEMORIES _____

_____
_____
_____
_____
_____
_____
_____

_____
_____
_____
_____
_____

FOOD I TASTED _____

_____
_____
_____

PLACE TO RECOMMEND _____

_____
_____
_____
_____
_____

my travel story

INTERESTING STORY HAPPENED TO ME

PLACE AND MEMORIES

_____
_____
_____
_____
_____
_____
_____

_____
_____
_____
_____

FOOD I TASTED

_____
_____
_____

PLACE TO RECOMMEND

_____
_____
_____
_____
_____

my travel story

INTERESTING STORY HAPPENED TO ME

my travel story

PLACE AND MEMORIES _____

_____
_____
_____
_____
_____
_____

FOOD I TASTED _____

_____
_____
_____

PLACE TO RECOMMEND _____

_____
_____
_____
_____

my travel story

INTERESTING STORY HAPPENED TO ME

my travel story

PLACE AND MEMORIES _____
_____
_____
_____
_____
_____
_____
_____
_____

_____
_____
_____
_____
_____

FOOD I TASTED _____
_____
_____
_____

PLACE TO RECOMMEND _____
_____
_____
_____
_____
_____
_____

my travel story

INTERESTING STORY HAPPENED TO ME

my travel story

PLACE AND MEMORIES _____

_____

_____

_____

_____

_____

_____

_____

_____

_____

_____

_____

FOOD I TASTED _____

_____

_____

_____

PLACE TO RECOMMEND _____

_____

_____

_____

_____

my travel story

INTERESTING STORY HAPPENED TO ME

my travel story

PLACE AND MEMORIES _____

_____

_____

_____

_____

_____

_____

_____

_____

_____

_____

_____

_____

FOOD I TASTED _____

_____

_____

_____

PLACE TO RECOMMEND _____

_____

_____

_____

_____

my travel story

INTERESTING STORY HAPPENED TO ME

my travel story

PLACE AND MEMORIES _____

_____

_____

_____

_____

_____

_____

_____

_____

_____

_____

_____

_____

_____

_____

FOOD I TASTED _____

_____

_____

_____

_____

PLACE TO RECOMMEND _____

_____

_____

_____

_____

my travel story

INTERESTING STORY HAPPENED TO ME

my travel story

PLACE AND MEMORIES _____
_____
_____
_____
_____
_____
_____
_____

FOOD I TASTED _____
_____
_____
_____
_____

PLACE TO RECOMMEND _____
_____
_____
_____
_____
_____

my travel story

INTERESTING STORY HAPPENED TO ME

PLACE AND MEMORIES _____

_____

_____

_____

_____

_____

_____

_____

_____

_____

_____

_____

_____

FOOD I TASTED _____

_____

_____

_____

PLACE TO RECOMMEND _____

_____

_____

_____

_____

my travel story

INTERESTING STORY HAPPENED TO ME

PLACE AND MEMORIES

_____
_____
_____
_____
_____
_____
_____
_____

FOOD I TASTED

_____
_____
_____

PLACE TO RECOMMEND

_____
_____
_____
_____

my travel story

INTERESTING STORY HAPPENED TO ME

PLACE AND MEMORIES _____

_____

_____

_____

_____

_____

_____

_____

_____

_____

_____

_____

_____

FOOD I TASTED _____

_____

_____

_____

PLACE TO RECOMMEND _____

_____

_____

_____

_____

_____

my travel story

INTERESTING STORY HAPPENED TO ME

PLACE AND MEMORIES _____

_____

_____

_____

_____

_____

_____

_____

_____

_____

_____

_____

_____

FOOD I TASTED _____

_____

_____

_____

PLACE TO RECOMMEND _____

_____

_____

_____

_____

_____

my travel story

INTERESTING STORY HAPPENED TO ME

PLACE AND MEMORIES _____

_____

_____

_____

_____

_____

_____

_____

_____

_____

_____

_____

_____

_____

FOOD I TASTED _____

_____

_____

_____

_____

PLACE TO RECOMMEND _____

_____

_____

_____

_____

_____

_____

my travel story

INTERESTING STORY HAPPENED TO ME

my travel story

PLACE AND MEMORIES _____

_____

_____

_____

_____

_____

_____

_____

_____

_____

_____

_____

_____

FOOD I TASTED _____

_____

_____

_____

PLACE TO RECOMMEND _____

_____

_____

_____

_____

_____

my travel story

INTERESTING STORY HAPPENED TO ME

my travel story

PLACE AND MEMORIES _____

_____

_____

_____

_____

_____

_____

_____

_____

_____

_____

_____

_____

_____

FOOD I TASTED _____

_____

_____

_____

PLACE TO RECOMMEND _____

_____

_____

_____

_____

_____

my travel story

INTERESTING STORY HAPPENED TO ME

PLACE AND MEMORIES

_____
_____
_____
_____
_____
_____
_____
_____
_____

_____
_____
_____
_____

FOOD I TASTED

_____
_____
_____
_____
_____

PLACE TO RECOMMEND

_____
_____
_____
_____
_____
_____
_____

my travel story

INTERESTING STORY HAPPENED TO ME

PLACE AND MEMORIES _____

_____
_____
_____
_____
_____
_____

_____
_____
_____
_____

FOOD I TASTED _____

_____
_____
_____

PLACE TO RECOMMEND _____

_____
_____
_____
_____
_____

my travel story

INTERESTING STORY HAPPENED TO ME

PLACE AND MEMORIES _____

_____
_____
_____
_____
_____
_____
_____

_____
_____
_____
_____

FOOD I TASTED _____

_____
_____
_____
_____

PLACE TO RECOMMEND _____

_____
_____
_____
_____
_____

my travel story

INTERESTING STORY HAPPENED TO ME

my travel story

PLACE AND MEMORIES _____

_____
_____
_____
_____
_____
_____
_____

_____
_____
_____
_____

FOOD I TASTED _____

_____
_____
_____

PLACE TO RECOMMEND _____

_____
_____
_____
_____
_____

my travel story

INTERESTING STORY HAPPENED TO ME

my travel story

PLACE AND MEMORIES _____
_____
_____
_____
_____
_____
_____
_____

_____
_____
_____
_____

FOOD I TASTED _____
_____
_____
_____

PLACE TO RECOMMEND _____
_____
_____
_____
_____
_____

my travel story

INTERESTING STORY HAPPENED TO ME

PLACE AND MEMORIES _____

_____

_____

_____

_____

_____

_____

_____

_____

_____

_____

_____

_____

_____

_____

FOOD I TASTED _____

_____

_____

_____

_____

PLACE TO RECOMMEND _____

_____

_____

_____

_____

_____

my travel story

INTERESTING STORY HAPPENED TO ME

PLACE AND MEMORIES _____
_____
_____
_____
_____
_____
_____
_____

_____
_____
_____
_____

FOOD I TASTED _____
_____
_____
_____

PLACE TO RECOMMEND _____
_____
_____
_____
_____

my travel story

INTERESTING STORY HAPPENED TO ME

my travel story

PLACE AND MEMORIES _____

_____
_____
_____
_____
_____
_____
_____

_____
_____
_____
_____
_____

FOOD I TASTED _____

_____
_____
_____

PLACE TO RECOMMEND _____

_____
_____
_____
_____
_____

my travel story

INTERESTING STORY HAPPENED TO ME

PLACE AND MEMORIES _____

_____
_____
_____
_____
_____
_____
_____

_____
_____
_____
_____
_____

FOOD I TASTED _____

_____
_____
_____
_____

PLACE TO RECOMMEND _____

_____
_____
_____
_____

my travel story

INTERESTING STORY HAPPENED TO ME

my travel story

PLACE AND MEMORIES _____

_____
_____
_____
_____
_____
_____
_____
_____
_____

_____
_____
_____
_____

FOOD I TASTED _____
_____
_____
_____
_____

PLACE TO RECOMMEND _____
_____
_____
_____
_____
_____

my travel story

INTERESTING STORY HAPPENED TO ME

PLACE AND MEMORIES _____

_____
_____
_____
_____
_____
_____
_____
_____

_____
_____
_____
_____

FOOD I TASTED _____
_____
_____
_____

PLACE TO RECOMMEND _____
_____
_____
_____
_____
_____

my travel story

INTERESTING STORY HAPPENED TO ME

PLACE AND MEMORIES _____

_____

_____

_____

_____

_____

_____

_____

_____

_____

_____

_____

_____

_____

FOOD I TASTED _____

_____

_____

_____

PLACE TO RECOMMEND _____

_____

_____

_____

_____

my travel story

INTERESTING STORY HAPPENED TO ME

my travel story

PLACE AND MEMORIES _____
_____
_____
_____
_____
_____
_____
_____

_____
_____
_____
_____
_____

FOOD I TASTED _____
_____
_____
_____
_____

PLACE TO RECOMMEND _____
_____
_____
_____
_____

my travel story

INTERESTING STORY HAPPENED TO ME

PLACE AND MEMORIES

_____
_____
_____
_____
_____
_____
_____
_____

_____
_____
_____
_____
_____

FOOD I TASTED

_____
_____
_____
_____

PLACE TO RECOMMEND

_____
_____
_____
_____
_____

my travel story

INTERESTING STORY HAPPENED TO ME

my travel story

PLACE AND MEMORIES _____

_____

_____

_____

_____

_____

_____

_____

_____

_____

_____

_____

_____

FOOD I TASTED _____

_____

_____

_____

PLACE TO RECOMMEND _____

_____

_____

_____

_____

_____

my travel story

INTERESTING STORY HAPPENED TO ME

PLACE AND MEMORIES _____

_____
_____
_____
_____
_____
_____
_____

_____
_____
_____
_____
_____

FOOD I TASTED _____

_____
_____
_____

PLACE TO RECOMMEND _____

_____
_____
_____
_____
_____
_____

my travel story

INTERESTING STORY HAPPENED TO ME

PLACE AND MEMORIES _____

_____
_____
_____
_____
_____
_____
_____

_____
_____
_____
_____
_____

FOOD I TASTED _____

_____
_____
_____
_____

PLACE TO RECOMMEND _____

_____
_____
_____
_____
_____

my travel story

INTERESTING STORY HAPPENED TO ME

my travel story

PLACE AND MEMORIES _____
_____
_____
_____
_____
_____
_____
_____

_____
_____
_____
_____

FOOD I TASTED _____
_____
_____
_____

PLACE TO RECOMMEND _____
_____
_____
_____
_____
_____

my travel story

INTERESTING STORY HAPPENED TO ME

my travel story

PLACE AND MEMORIES _____
_____
_____
_____
_____
_____
_____
_____

_____
_____
_____
_____
_____

FOOD I TASTED _____
_____
_____
_____
_____

PLACE TO RECOMMEND _____
_____
_____
_____
_____
_____
_____

my travel story

INTERESTING STORY HAPPENED TO ME

my travel story

PLACE AND MEMORIES _____

_____
_____
_____
_____
_____
_____
_____

_____
_____
_____
_____

FOOD I TASTED _____
_____
_____
_____
_____

PLACE TO RECOMMEND _____
_____
_____
_____
_____
_____

my travel story

INTERESTING STORY HAPPENED TO ME

PLACE AND MEMORIES _____

_____
_____
_____
_____
_____
_____
_____

_____
_____
_____
_____

FOOD I TASTED _____

_____
_____
_____
_____

PLACE TO RECOMMEND _____

_____
_____
_____
_____
_____

my travel story

INTERESTING STORY HAPPENED TO ME

my travel story

PLACE AND MEMORIES _____

_____

_____

_____

_____

_____

_____

_____

_____

_____

_____

_____

_____

FOOD I TASTED _____

_____

_____

_____

PLACE TO RECOMMEND _____

_____

_____

_____

_____

_____

my travel story

INTERESTING STORY HAPPENED TO ME

my travel story

PLACE AND MEMORIES _____

_____
_____
_____
_____
_____
_____
_____

_____
_____
_____
_____
_____

FOOD I TASTED _____

_____
_____
_____
_____

PLACE TO RECOMMEND _____

_____
_____
_____
_____
_____

my travel story

INTERESTING STORY HAPPENED TO ME

PLACE AND MEMORIES _____
_____
_____
_____
_____
_____
_____
_____

_____
_____
_____
_____

FOOD I TASTED _____
_____
_____
_____
_____

PLACE TO RECOMMEND _____
_____
_____
_____
_____
_____
_____

my travel story

INTERESTING STORY HAPPENED TO ME

PLACE AND MEMORIES _____

_____

_____

_____

_____

_____

_____

_____

_____

_____

_____

_____

_____

FOOD I TASTED _____

_____

_____

_____

PLACE TO RECOMMEND _____

_____

_____

_____

_____

_____

my travel story

Made in the USA
Monee, IL
19 May 2022

96689333R00065